The Safari Series

Henry the Hyena Loses His Giggle

Story by Ian Pletzer

Illustrations by Joni-Leigh Doran

Editing by Narina Exelby. Internal book design and cover design by Joni-leigh Doran.

ISBN - 978-0-620-83172-7

This book is dedicated to the future conservationists of the world.

About Ian and Joni-Leigh

Combining their deep appreciation of wildlife with a calling to educate children about the responsibility of conservation, nature guide Ian and illustrator Joni-Leigh use adorable animal characters to highlight their importance to the planet and combine these messages with small life lessons related to personal development.

The Safari Series

Henry the Hyena Loses His Giggle

Henry was a spotted hyena. He lived on the wild plains of the African savannah.

When Henry was happy, which was most of the time, he giggled. You see, being a hyena was a really good life.

By day, Henry slept lazily in the cool shade of a termite mound, and by night he wandered around the African bush looking for scraps of food to eat.

One beautiful evening just before sunset, Henry was walking past a safari vehicle full of humans.

He heard the field guide say that hyenas are so ugly that they form part of the Ugly Five; together with the wildebeest, the warthog, the maribou stork and the lappet-faced vulture.

The people on the truck all pointed at Henry and laughed. Poor Henry suddenly felt very ashamed.

When Henry woke the next morning, his giggle was gone. He was feeling very sad, so he went to find his friend Willie the Wildebeest.

“Hi Willie, do you know that we are part of the Ugly Five?”

“*Gnuuu*,” said Willie. “I don’t care about that silly group. All I care about is following the rains to find good grazing. And to watch out for hungry lions of course! Pay no attention to the silly humans, Henry.”

But Henry wasn't satisfied, so he decided to pay a visit to Walter the warthog. He found Walter rolling around in a mud wallow.

"Hey Walter, do you know we are part of the Ugly Five?"

"*Snort*," said Walter. "Why should I care about that? These warts on my face are to protect me from fighting. I need them, or I would *really* look ugly! Besides, I am happily married with lots of little piglets. I am too busy protecting them to care about what the silly humans think!"

The next day, Henry followed Larry the lappet-faced vulture to a leftover kill.
Mark the marabou stork was also there.

"Hi Guys," said Henry.
"Do you know, we are part of the Ugly Five?"

"*Kraakkaa*," said Larry.
"*Skekkeekkee*," said Mark.

"We have an important job to do!" they sqauwked.

“We are the cleaners. We find the leftover carcasses and eat up the old meat and scraps to prevent diseases from spreading,” said Larry.

“It’s not a pretty job, but someone has to do it. It may be ugly work, but it’s very, very important,” said Mark.

“Don’t worry about what people think or say, Henry. There will always be those who judge you... And *that* is ugly,” they said in unison.

So after gnawing on a bone and playing his part in the ecosystem, Henry felt better.

And as he scampered home he let out a whoop! And guess what? Henry found his giggle!